WINTER
Phonemic Awareness Songs & Rhymes

♪ Fun Lyrics Sung to Familiar Tunes ♫

• Written by •

Kimberly Jordano & Trisha Callella-Jones

Editor: Kristine Johnson

Illustrator: Darcy Tom

Project Director: Carolea Williams

Table of Contents

What Will We Wear?

SONGS

ACTIVITIES

Happy Holidays

SONGS

ACTIVITIES

Introduction

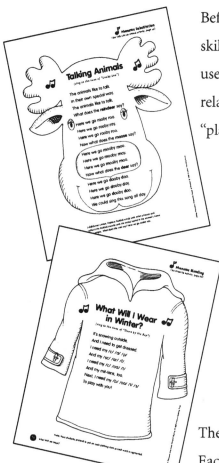

Before children learn to read words in print, they must develop the important skill of auditory discrimination—an awareness of how letters and words are used in oral language. *Phonemic Awareness Songs & Rhymes* provides theme-related songs and activities that encourage children to manipulate sounds and "play with language." Children learn to

- *listen for and identify rhyming words.*
- *identify words that include the same sound.*
- *listen for and count syllables within a word.*
- *identify the beginning, middle, and ending sounds in words.*
- *count and clap out the number of sounds in words.*
- *combine letter sounds to form words.*
- *divide words into separate sounds.*
- *match sounds to letters of the alphabet.*

The activities and songs in this resource are both easy to use and fun to do. Each reproducible activity card and song sheet clearly identifies the phonemic-awareness task(s) being reinforced. The cards and song sheets also indicate which songs and activities can be taught together. *Phonemic Awareness Songs & Rhymes* also includes supplementary reproducibles and a helpful cross-check index to simplify lesson preparations. If you are unfamiliar with any of the tunes, simply chant the song as a rhyme. This is an all-in-one resource filled with fun, interactive activities and silly, playful songs—a winning combination for any reading-development program!

What Is Phonemic Awareness?

Phonemic awareness is the ability to recognize and manipulate individual sound units (phonemes) in spoken language: to examine language independent of meaning, to see relationships between sounds in words, and to rearrange sounds to create new words. For example, the word *chick* is made up of three phonemes (/ch/ /i/ /k/*); it can be changed to the word *pick* by replacing /ch/ with /p/.

Students who are phonemically aware are able to master the following tasks:

Rhyming—The ability to identify and form rhyming words.

    Example: Do these words rhyme?

                  fun—fan   *no*

                  pig—wig   *yes*

                  cheer—year   *yes*

                  bread—seed   *no*

Sound Matching—The ability to hear and identify similar word patterns.

    Example: Which word does not belong?

                  sun, sad, sip, tub   *tub*

                  mat, bat, hop, cat   *hop*

                  bee, meat, sea, fee   *meat*

* When letters appear between slash marks (such as /k/), the sound rather than the letter name is represented.

Syllable Counting—The ability to
identify the number of syllables in
spoken words.

    Example: How many syllables do
           you hear in these
           words?

ticket	*2*
dog	*1*
bicycle	*3*
pencil	*2*

Syllable Splitting—The ability to identify onsets and rimes.*

    Example: What word do you have when you join these
           sounds together?

j–ump	*jump*
t–an	*tan*
cl–imb	*climb*
str–eet	*street*

Phoneme Blending—The ability to orally blend individual sounds to form
a word.

    Example: What word do you have when you join these sounds together?

/m/ /a/ /p/	*map*
/j/ /a/ /k/	*jack*
/ch/ /ee/ /p/	*cheap*
/b/ /r/ /o/ /k/	*broke*

* An *onset* is all the sounds in a word that come before the first vowel. A *rime* is the first
vowel in a word and all the sounds that follow. (For example, in the word *splash*, the onset is
spl- and the rime is *-ash*.)

Phoneme Isolation—The ability to identify the beginning, middle, and ending sounds in a word.

Examples:

What's the beginning sound in *toe*?   /t/

What's the middle sound in *big*?   /i/

What's the ending sound in *plane*?   /n/

Phoneme Counting—The ability to count the number of phonemes in a word.

Example: How many sounds do you hear in these words?

at   *2*

lake   *3*

paint   *4*

tent   *4*

Phoneme Segmentation—The ability to break apart a word into individual sounds.

Example: Which sounds do you hear in these words?

mud   /m/ /u/ /d/

play   /p/ /l/ /a/

strike   /s/ /t/ /r/ /i/ /k/

Phoneme Addition—The ability to add a beginning, middle, or ending sound to a word.

Examples:

$$p + lay = play$$
$$grew + m = groom$$

What word would you have if you added /b/ to the beginning of *low?*   *blow*

What word would you have if you added /r/ to the middle of *bed?*   *bread*

What word would you have if you added /s/ to the end of *how?*   *house*

Phoneme Deletion—The ability to omit the beginning, middle, or ending sound from a word.

Examples:

What word would you have if you took out the /f/ in *flake?*   *lake*

What word would you have if you took out the /l/ in *play?*   *pay*

What word would you have if you took out the /t/ in *meat?*   *me*

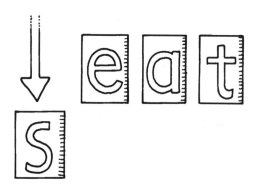

Phoneme Substitution—The ability to substitute a new sound for the beginning, middle, or ending sound of a word.

Examples:

What word would you have if you changed the /b/ in *ball* to a /t/?   *tall*

What word would you have if you changed the /o/ in *hot* to an /a/?   *hat*

What word would you have if you changed the /p/ in *map* to a /d/?   *mad*

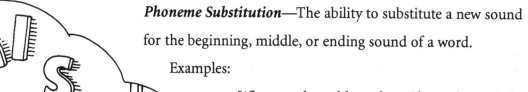

Make the Most of It!

The songs and rhymes in this resource help lay a foundation for phonics instruction in a fun and exciting way. Use them when teaching specific phonemic-awareness tasks (see the song titles listed on individual activity cards), or follow the suggestions below to incorporate these "kid-captivating" songs and rhymes into your core curriculum.

Song Cards

Enlarge, decorate, and laminate each song for daily shared reading and singing. Use "magic wands" or theme-related reading sticks to point to the words as students sing the songs. Make a fun, accessible display by using clothespins to hang the song sheets from a plastic toy chain, or store the song sheets in baskets for use at a center or for free-choice reading time.

Individual Songbooks

Provide each student with a three-pronged folder. As a new song is learned, give each child a photocopy of the song sheet to decorate, read, sing, and then add to his or her notebook. Provide weekly opportunities for students to reread and sing their favorite songs. Send the notebooks home at Open House or at the end of the year for students to share with their families.

Songs on Tape

Practice singing the songs with your students. Once students are familiar with a song, use a tape recorder to make a class tape of the song. Place copies of the song sheets and the cassette at a listening center for students to use.

Rhyme Time

I'm thinking of some words
  that rhyme with [dog.]
I know one word
  that rhymes is [   ].
What other rhyming words
  could there be?
Think about it, then
  quickly tell me!

Charts

Copy the songs onto large individual sheets of chart paper. Use different colored markers to write key words or sounds. Invite students to "frame" the key words with their hands or with Wikki Stix (available at teacher-supply stores), use a reading stick to point to the words, highlight key words with highlighters or highlighting tape (found at most office-supply stores), or cover words with sticky notes. For additional learning and fun, add to the chart related pictures or reproducible picture cards from the back of this resource.

Big Books

Write each line from one of the songs on a separate sheet of large construction paper. Invite students to draw pictures on the construction paper that correspond to each line. Bind pages into a class big book and display it in the class library for students to reread.

I left my cave looking for some honey, But all I found was a whole lot of money!

Photo Name Cards

Take a photograph of each child and of any classroom pets or puppets. Write each student's name on an index card, a sentence strip, or a tongue depressor, and then attach his or her photo to it. Place the photo name cards in a pocket chart or hold them up while you sing name-recognition songs.

Fluffy

Adam

Hannah

Puppets

Make reduced copies of a song sheet, glue them to the backs of individual paper lunch sacks, and distribute them to students. Have students draw favorite song-related characters on the front of their sack to make paper-sack puppets. Invite the class to use the hand puppets while singing and dramatizing the corresponding song written on the back.

Flannel Board

Cover the song lyrics on the song sheet with paper, photocopy the song-sheet artwork onto card stock, and color the images. Photocopy any picture cards from the back of this resource that correspond to the song, cut them out, and color them. Invite students to draw pictures that correspond to the song, and then photocopy the pictures onto card stock. Glue felt or attach Velcro to the back of the card stock. Invite students to manipulate the images on a flannel board while singing the song.

Magnetic Board

Magnetic boards include cookie sheets, oven-burner covers, and magnetic chalkboards. Photocopy on card stock picture cards from the back of this resource, cut them out, and color them. Write song lyrics on sentence strips and alphabet letters on index cards. Add magnetic tape to the backs of the sentence strips, picture cards, and letter cards. Invite students to manipulate the images or letters on the magnetic board while singing the song.

Storyboards

Invite students to create a construction-paper backdrop that represents a scene from a song. Have students draw pictures, cut them out, and glue some of them directly on the backdrop to make a storyboard. Invite students to glue other pictures to craft sticks to be used as pointers or puppets while singing.

Music and Movement

March around the room with students while singing one of the songs. For extra fun, give students pom-poms and/or musical instruments to use while they sing. Ask a volunteer to "be the teacher" and point to each word on the song chart. Allow students to sing solos or duets in front of the class.

Themes and Topics

Enrich your studies by placing a copy of the song sheet on the back of theme-related projects, bulletin boards, illustrated wall stories, artwork, or class big books. Use the songs to introduce new units and to generate ideas for artwork.

Card Sorting

Place in a pocket chart picture cards from the back of this resource. Invite students to sort the picture cards by various categories, such as initial sound, final sound, rhyming pairs, number of sounds, or number of syllables. For additional learning, place the picture cards in a learning center for students to re-sort.

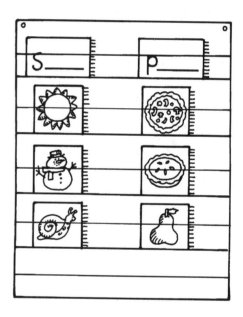

Rhyming March

Have students place their chairs in a circle. Place on the chairs picture cards from the back of this resource, and then have students march around the chairs while singing one of the songs. When the music stops, have students say a word that rhymes with the picture card next to them. Remind students that rhyming words can be nonsense words, too.

Reading Strategies

Write the lines of one of the songs on sentence strips and distribute them to different students. Also distribute any picture cards from the back of this resource if they correspond with the song. While singing the song, invite students to place their sentence strip or picture card in the appropriate place in the pocket chart. Prompt students with reading-strategy questions such as

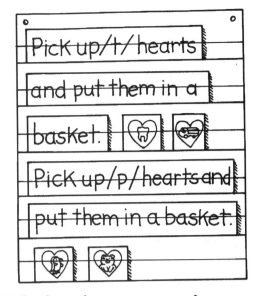

What sound do you hear at the beginning of _____? What letter do you expect to see? Does that make sense, sound right, and look right? What would the first letter of the sentence look like? What do you expect to see at the end of the sentence? How many letters are in the word _____? How many words are in the sentence?

Sentence Manipulation

Write the lines of a song on sentence strips and then cut apart the strips into words or phrases. Write some consonants on index cards for students to substitute different phonemes. Invite students to rebuild or manipulate the song.

Jump Rope Chants

Invite students to jump rope or bounce a ball while chanting the songs. The steady beat of the jump rope will help children keep the rhyming pattern. Challenge students to continue jumping rope or bouncing the ball throughout an entire song.

Unscramble the Word

Print in large letters on a sentence strip a key word from one of the songs. Cut apart the letters, and pass out each letter to a different student. Invite students to bring their letter to the pocket chart and reassemble the word.

Be the Word

Write letters on separate index cards and distribute the cards to students. Call out a word from a song and invite students who have a letter from that word to stand in the correct order to "be," or rebuild, the word. To "be" the sentence, write words from a song on separate index cards and pass them out. Have students stand in the correct order to rebuild the sentence.

Word Families

Use magnetic letters on a magnetic surface to spell a common rhyming word, such as *cat.* Invite students to replace the first letter of the word with another to form additional rhyming words, such as *bat, hat,* and *sat.* Extend learning by having students spell out high-frequency words used in the song lyrics.

Magic Reading Sticks

To make reading sticks for pointing to song lyrics while chanting or singing, have students dip the ends of chopsticks into brightly colored paint and sprinkle them with glitter. Invite students to tie ribbons to their "magical" reading stick. Create more reading sticks by using a hot glue gun to attach to dowels plastic animals or other small toys that correspond with subjects in the songs.

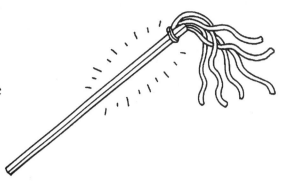

Word Hunts

Cut out a rectangular hole in the center of several brightly colored flyswatters so that when the fly-swatters are placed over a word on a chart or a sentence strip, the word is framed. (Cut some holes longer than others so different-size words can be framed.) Invite a student to come to a chart or pocket chart and "hunt" for a word. For example, have a student hunt for a word that rhymes with *hair* and begins with /b/. The student then frames the word *bear* using the flyswatter.

Magic Reading Glasses

Collect inexpensive plastic toy glasses (available at party-supply stores), and punch out the lenses. Add curling ribbon to the sides of each pair for a fun decoration. Place the glasses in a special place for students to wear while reading.

Very Special Visors

Collect a few plastic visors. Decorate the visors with puffy paint and glitter glue. Invite a "leader of the day" to wear the visor and choose a favorite song for the class to sing.

♫ Rhyme Time ♫

(sing to the tune of "I'm Bringing Home a Baby Bumblebee")

This is a song that's called "Rhyme Time."
I'll say a word, then you tell me a rhyme.
Let's see how many rhymes we know.
On your mark, get ready, let's go!

I'm thinking of some words that rhyme with **dog.**
I know one word that rhymes is **frog.**
What other rhyming words could there be?
Think about it, then quickly tell me!

wig

Pig

bee

tree

hat

cat

one

sun

frog

dog

house

mouse

lamp

stamp

USA 32

Additional verses: Invite students to shout out other words that rhyme with the bolded words. Then, replace bolded words with other rhyming words to continue the song. For example, *I'm thinking of some words that rhyme with* **pig.** *I know one word that rhymes is* **wig.**

Winter Phonemic Awareness Songs & Rhymes © 1998 Creative Teaching Press

♫ Where Is the Sound? ♫

(sing to the tune of "Where, Oh, Where Has My Little Dog Gone?")

Where, oh, where do you hear the **/ch/** sound?

Where, oh, where can it be?

Is it the first, the middle, or at the end?

Where, oh, where can it be?

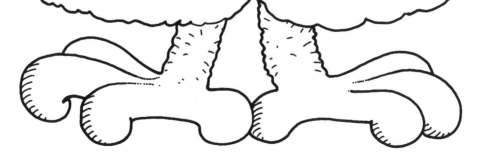

Note: Call out a word that has the bolded sound somewhere in the word, and have students shout out where the sound is. For example, /ch/ is the first sound in *chicken* and the last sound in *peach*.

Additional verses: Replace the bolded sound with other sounds to continue the song.

♫ Song Changes ♫

(sing to the tune of "Deck the Halls")

Sing a song that changes first sounds,

La la la la la, la la la la.

Sing the song with the **/w/** sound.

Wa wa wa wa wa, wa wa wa wa.

Winter and **weather** start with **/w/.**

Wa wa wa, wa wa wa, wa, wa, wa.

Change it back to /l/ again.

La la la la la, la la la la.

Sing a song that changes last sounds,

La la la la la, la la la la.

Sing the song with the **/oo/** sound.

Loo loo loo loo loo, loo loo loo loo.

Igloo and **emu** end with **/oo/.**

Loo loo loo, loo loo loo, loo, loo, loo.

Change it back to /a/ again.

La la la la la, la la la la.

Additional verses: Replace the bolded sounds and words to continue the song.
For example, *Sing the song with the /h/ sound. Ha ha ha ha ha, ha ha ha ha.*
Happy and ***holiday*** start with ***/h/.*** Or, *Sing the song with the /ay/ sound. Lay
lay lay lay lay, lay lay lay lay.* ***Ballet*** and ***sleigh*** end with ***/ay/.***

Winter Phonemic Awareness Songs & Rhymes © 1998 Creative Teaching Press

♫ 'Round the Circle ♫

(sing to the tune of "Pop! Goes the Weasel")

'Round and 'round the circle you go.
Where you'll stop, we don't know.
If your name starts with the same sound,
Then you sit down on the ground.

Note: Have a volunteer walk around a circle and stop in front of one child. All children whose names begin with the same sound as that child sit on the ground.
Additional verses: Invite another student to walk around the circle for the next round. Continue singing until all students are seated.

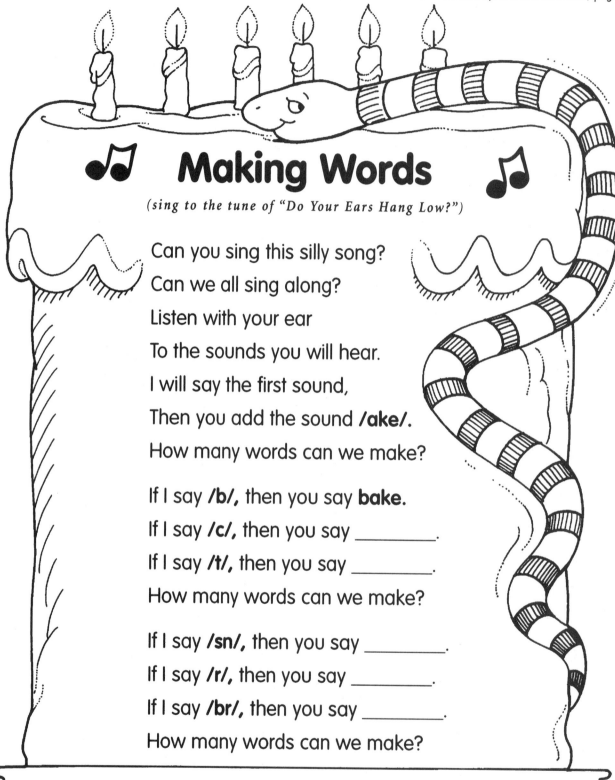

Making Words

(sing to the tune of "Do Your Ears Hang Low?")

Can you sing this silly song?

Can we all sing along?

Listen with your ear

To the sounds you will hear.

I will say the first sound,

Then you add the sound **/ake/.**

How many words can we make?

If I say **/b/,** then you say **bake.**

If I say **/c/,** then you say _____.

If I say **/t/,** then you say _____.

How many words can we make?

If I say **/sn/,** then you say _____.

If I say **/r/,** then you say _____.

If I say **/br/,** then you say _____.

How many words can we make?

Note: Pause for students to say the new word at the end of each line.

Additional verses: Replace the beginning sounds with other onsets to continue the song. For example, *If I say /sh/, then you say shake. If I say /w/, then you say _____. If I say /st/, then you say _____.* Replace the rime */ake/* to vary the song. For example, *Then you add the sound /ing/. How many words can we sing? If I say /k/, then you say king. If I say /st/ then you say _____.*

♫ Oobie-Oobie ♫

(sing to the tune of "John Jacob Jingleheimer Schmidt")

We love to sing this silly song.

Oobie oobie oobie oobie oo.

When we go out to play,

Our friends will always say,

"Let's sing a song with the sound **/ch/**."

Choobie, **ch**oobie, **ch**oobie.

We love to sing this silly song,

Choobie **ch**oobie **ch**oobie **ch**oobie **ch**oo.

When we go out to play,

Our friends will always say,

"Let's sing a song with the sound **/g/**."

Goobie, **g**oobie, **g**oobie.

We love to sing this silly song,

Goobie **g**oobie **g**oobie **g**oobie **g**oo.

When we go out to play,

Our friends will always say,

"Let's sing a song with the sound **/t/**."

Toobie, **t**oobie, **t**oobie.

Additional verses: Replace the bolded sounds to continue the song.

Winter Phonemic Awareness Songs & Rhymes © 1998 Creative Teaching Press

🎵 First and Last Sounds 🎵

(sing to the tune of "Are You Sleeping?")

What's the first sound,
What's the first sound,
In **Sarah,**
In **Sarah?**

/S/ is the first sound,
/S/ is the first sound,
In **Sarah,**
In **Sarah.**

What's the last sound,
What's the last sound,
In **Jeffrey,**
In **Jeffrey?**

/EE/ is the last sound,
/EE/ is the last sound,
In **Jeffrey,**
In **Jeffrey.**

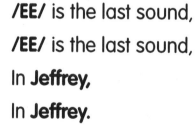

Additional verses: Replace the bolded names and sounds to continue the song.

Winter Phonemic Awareness Songs & Rhymes © 1998 Creative Teaching Press

♪ **Rhyming**
(See Teddy Bear Day and Pass the
Polar Bear activities, page 30)

♫ Teddy Likes to Rhyme ♫

(sing to the tune of "Pop! Goes the Weasel")

Teddy bear has so much fun
In any kind of weather.
See if you can guess what he does
So you can play together.

Teddy likes to play outside
And it rhymes with **hike.**
What do you think he wants to do?
Teddy wants to **bike!**

Teddy likes to play outside
And it rhymes with **fall.**
What do you think he wants to do?
Teddy wants to play **ball!**

Teddy likes to play outside
And it rhymes with **fun.**
What do you think he wants to do?
Teddy wants to **run!**

Additional verses: Replace the bolded words with
rhyming words to continue the song. For example, *Teddy
likes to play outside and it rhymes with **locker.** What do
you think he wants to do? Teddy wants to play **soccer!***

Clap the Beats

(sing to the tune of "The Farmer in the Dell")

Can you clap the beats?

Can you clap the beats?

Listen to the name I say,

And help me clap the beats.

Kim-ber-ly.

Kim-ber-ly.

How many beats do you hear in **Kim-ber-ly?**

Can you clap the beats?

Can you clap the beats?

Listen to the name I say,

And help me clap the beats.

Tri-sha.

Tri-sha.

How many beats do you hear in **Tri-sha?**

Additional verses: Replace the bolded names with your students' names to continue the song.

Zip-a-Zee-Zoo-Zah

(sing to the tune of "Zip-a-Dee-Doo-Dah")

Zip-a-**z**ee-**z**oo-**z**ah,

Zip-a-**z**ee-**z**ay.

I love to sing this song every day.

Zip-a-**z**ee-**z**oo-**z**ah,

Zip-a-**z**ee-**z**ay.

Come along and sing in this silly way.

Bip-a-**b**ee-**b**oo-**b**ah,

Bip-a-**b**ee-**b**ay.

I love to sing this song every day.

Bip-a-**b**ee-**b**oo-**b**ah,

Bip-a-**b**ee-**b**ay.

Come along and sing in this silly way.

Ship-a-**sh**ee-**sh**oo-**sh**ah,

Ship-a-**sh**ee-**sh**ay.

I love to sing this song every day.

Ship-a-**sh**ee-**sh**oo-**sh**ah,

Ship-a-**sh**ee-**sh**ay.

Let's sing together in this silly way.

Additional verses: Replace the bolded sounds to continue the song. For example, *Dip-a-dee-doo-dah, dip-a-dee-day.*

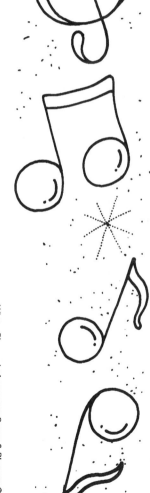

Rhyming Headbands

Rhyming

Materials

- "Rhyme Time" song (page 16)
- Rhyming Picture Cards (pages 83 and 84)
- scissors
- crayons or markers
- stapler
- sentence strips

Photocopy the Rhyming Picture Cards, cut the cards apart, and give each student one card to decorate. Staple each student's card onto separate sentence strips to make headbands. As the class sings "Rhyme Time," ask students wearing the rhyming picture card to pop up. Invite students to illustrate additional rhyming words and add them to the headbands.

(*Use with "Rhyme Time," page 16*)

Find the Sound

Phoneme Isolation

Materials

- Polar Bear reproducible (page 85)
- fish crackers

Have each student place a fish cracker on a photocopy of the Polar Bear reproducible. Ask students to isolate beginning, middle, and ending sounds in words as they slowly slide the fish cracker across the animal's body and slowly say the word. Have students stop moving the cracker when they say the sound you are asking them to locate.

(*Use with "Where Is the Sound?" page 17*)

Sing It Again

Sound Matching, Phoneme Isolation, Phoneme Addition, Phoneme Deletion

Place magnetic letters in a sack and select a volunteer to draw out a letter. Brainstorm words that begin or end with the same sound as the letter and write them on the board. Then sing "Song Changes," replacing the bolded words and sounds with the new ones. For added fun, invite a volunteer to play a xylophone while the class sings the *La la la la la, la la la la* part.

(Use with "Song Changes," page 18)

Materials

- "Song Changes" song (page 18)
- magnetic letters
- sack
- xylophone

Spin and Sing

Sound Matching, Phoneme Counting

Have students stand in a circle. Distribute to each student a picture card or object representing no more than five different sounds. Choose a volunteer to stand in the middle with eyes closed and spin around while pointing a finger. Have students sing "'Round the Circle." When the song is over, the spinning child stops, names the picture or object that he or she is pointing to, and counts the number of phonemes in the word. Then all students who hold a picture or an object that begins with the same sound sit down. For example, if the volunteer points to a child holding a picture of a mouse, the volunteer says *mouse, three* (because mouse has three phonemes—/m/ /ou/ /s/), and all students who have a picture that begins with /m/ sit down. Continue playing until all students are seated.

(Use with "'Round the Circle," page 19)

Materials

- "'Round the Circle" song (page 19)
- picture cards or small objects

Moose has 3 sounds. /m//oo//s/

The Sound Families
Phoneme Blending, Phoneme Addition

Materials

- "Making Words" song (page 20)
- sentence strips
- pocket chart
- large index cards

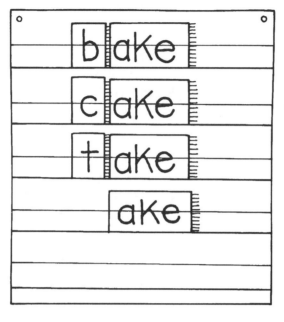

Write *ake* in large letters on sentence strips and place them in a pocket chart. Write on large index cards the letters *b, br, c, f, fl, l, m, qu, r, s, sh, sn, st, t,* and *w,* and distribute them to students. While singing "Making Words," have students place the correct beginning sound in the pocket chart to form the new word. To extend the activity, replace the rime *ake* with another rime such as *ack, ide,* or *eet.* Invite students to add onsets to create words such as *back, bride,* or *feet.*

(Use with "Making Words," page 20)

Spell It Out
Phoneme Substitution

Materials

- large index cards

Write on large index cards the letters *a, b, c, e, f, k, l, m, qu, r, s, t,* and *w,* and distribute them to students. Say a word ending with the sound *ake,* and have students stand at the front of the class and arrange themselves in the correct order to spell the word. Next, tell them to change one letter to make a new word. For example, if the first word was *rake,* have students change one letter to make the word *lake.* The student with *l* would replace the student with *r.* Then ask the class to say the new word aloud. Invite the class to help determine who will sit down and who needs to come to the front of the room to spell the new word.

(Use with "Making Words," page 20)

Let's Line Up
Phoneme Substitution

Write the words to the first verse of "Oobie-Oobie" on sentence strips and display them in a pocket chart. Write on separate sentence strips different long and short vowels. Instead of adding a new consonant sound, invite students to replace the vowel sound in the song. Replace the *oo* to change the song. For example, *Eebie eebie eebie eebie ee* or *Ibie ibie ibie ibie i*. Sing the song with consonant changes as students leave for lunch or recess. Have students listen for the first sound in their name as a cue to line up. Lining up was never so much fun!

(Use with "Oobie-Oobie," page 21)

Materials

● "Oobie-Oobie" song (page 21)

● sentence strips

● pocket chart

Friend Sound Sort
Phoneme Isolation

Glue student photos to index cards and place them in a pocket chart. Sing "First and Last Sounds" with your class. Have students sort the photo cards by initial or final sound. Ask questions such as *Are there more students with the first sound /t/ or /ch/?* or *Who has the most letter Ss in their name?*

(Use with "First and Last Sounds," page 22)

Materials

● "First and Last Sounds" song (page 22)

● glue

● student photos

● index cards

● pocket chart

Teddy Bear Day

Rhyming

Celebrate a special Teddy Bear Day with your class. Invite students to bring to class their favorite stuffed bear. Brainstorm with students actions they think their teddy bears might want to do and words that rhyme with those actions. While singing "Teddy Likes to Rhyme," have students act out the movements with their own bears.

(Use with "Teddy Likes to Rhyme," page 23)

Materials

- "Teddy Likes to Rhyme" song (page 23)

- stuffed bears (brought from home)

Pass the Polar Bear

Rhyming

Materials

- stuffed polar bear

- music

Bring in a stuffed polar bear. Have students sit in a circle. Pass the bear around the circle while playing background music. When the music stops, the student holding the bear says a word that rhymes with *bear*. Challenge students not to repeat any of the words already said. To continue the game, invite students to change the rhyming word from *bear* to other easy-to-rhyme winter words such as *white, snows, deer, sleigh, rain, skied,* or *blew.*

(Use with "Teddy Likes to Rhyme," page 23)

Play the Beats
Syllable Counting

Glue student photos to index cards and place them in a hat, mitten, or basket. Choose a photo card and show it to the class. Have students clap and count the syllables in that student's name. For added fun, distribute musical instruments such as rhythm sticks or drums to the class. Instead of clapping the beats, have students play the beats of each name on their instrument.

(Use with "Clap the Beats," page 24)

(Use with "Clap the Beats," page 24)

Man-dy

Stick a Letter
Phoneme Substitution

Choose a student to pick a magnetic letter from a special bag or basket. Invite the student to place the letter on a metal surface. Sing "Zip-a-Zee-Zoo-Zah" with the class, substituting the first sound with the sound that letter makes.

(Use with "Zip-a-Zee-Zoo-Zah," page 25)

(Use with "Zip-a-Zee-Zoo-Zah," page 25)

Materials

- glue
- student photos
- index cards
- hat, mitten, or basket
- musical instruments (optional)

Materials

- "Zip-a-Zee-Zoo-Zah" song (page 25)
- bag or basket with magnetic letters
- metal surface such as a cookie sheet or magnetic board

♪ Phoneme Substitution
(See Polar Play activity, page 40)

Who Can Find the Polar Bear?

(sing to the tune of "Someone's in the Kitchen with Dinah")

Who can find the polar bear?

Who can find the polar bear?

Who can find the polar bear

Playing in the snow today?

The seal said,

"Se, si, siddley-i-o,

Se, si, siddley-i-o-o-o-o.

Se, si, where did he go?

Run and ask our friend penguin."

The penguin said,

"Pe, pi, piddley-i-o,

Pe, pi, piddley-i-o-o-o-o.

Pe, pi, where did he go?

Run and ask our friend whale."

The whale said,

"We, wi, widdley-i-o,

We, wi, widdley-i-o-o-o-o.

We, wi, I think I know.

Just follow his footprints."

Little Brown Bear

(sing to the tune of "Little White Duck")

I'm a little brown bear
Looking for some honey.
Little brown bear
Looking kind of funny.
I left my cave looking for some **trees,**
But all I found were some **honeybees!**
I'm a little brown bear
Looking for some honey.
Ouch! Ouch! Ouch!

Additional verses: Replace the bolded words with other rhyming words to continue the song. For example, *I left my cave looking for some **rocks,** but all I found were some **dirty old socks!***

Arctic Pals

(sing to the tune of "Alouette")

Polly Penguin

Walking through the Arctic

Eating pasta, pears, and pie.

She eats foods that start with /p/.

Can you name some foods she'll eat?

Sally Seal

Walking through the Arctic

Singing about sun, surf, and sky.

She sings words that start with /s/.

Can you name some songs she'll sing?

Bobby Bear

Walking through the Arctic

Playing with balls, bats, and balloons.

He plays games that start with /b/.

Can you name some games he'll play?

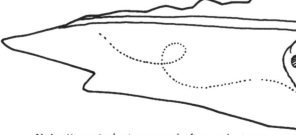

Note: Have students respond after each stanza.

Winter Phonemic Awareness Songs & Rhymes © 1998 Creative Teaching Press

♫ Antarctica Riddles ♫

(sing to the tune of "Wheels on the Bus")

I live in the ocean, and I like to swim,
I like to swim, I like to swim.
I live in the ocean, and I like to swim.
My name rhymes with **pail.**

I like to catch fish to feed my chicks,
Feed my chicks, feed my chicks.
I like to catch fish to feed my chicks.
My name rhymes with **Ben Gwen.**

I am big and strong, furry and white,
Furry and white, furry and white.
I am big and strong, furry and white.
My name rhymes with **molar hair.**

I have flippers that help me swim,
Help me swim, help me swim.
I have flippers that help me swim.
My name rhymes with **wheel.**

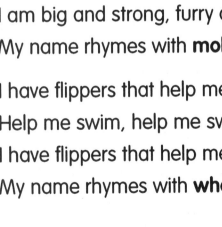

Note: Have students shout the animal name after each stanza.

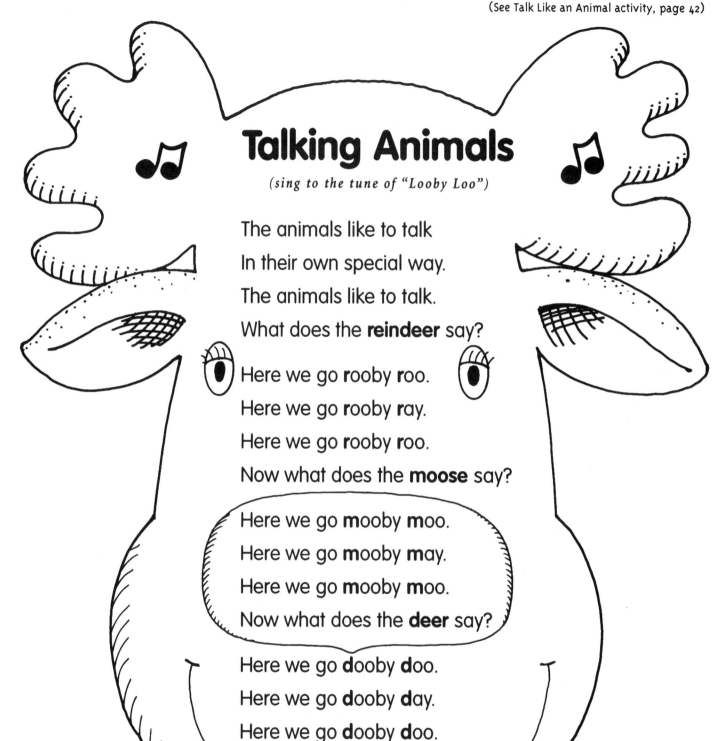

Talking Animals

(sing to the tune of "Looby Loo")

The animals like to talk

In their own special way.

The animals like to talk.

What does the **reindeer** say?

Here we go **r**ooby **r**oo.

Here we go **r**ooby **r**ay.

Here we go **r**ooby **r**oo.

Now what does the **moose** say?

Here we go **m**ooby **m**oo.

Here we go **m**ooby **m**ay.

Here we go **m**ooby **m**oo.

Now what does the **deer** say?

Here we go **d**ooby **d**oo.

Here we go **d**ooby **d**ay.

Here we go **d**ooby **d**oo.

We could sing this song all day.

Additional verses: Replace bolded words with other animals and
replace the bolded sounds with the initial sound in the animal's name.
For example, *What does the **seal** say? Here we go sooby soo.*

Winter Phonemic Awareness Songs & Rhymes © 1998 Creative Teaching Press

♫ The Mitten ♫

(sing to the tune of "The Farmer in the Dell")

The **mole** is in the mitten.
The **mole** is in the mitten.
Mi-mo the **m**erry-o,
The **mole** is in the mitten.

The **rabbit** is in the mitten.
The **rabbit** is in the mitten.
Ri-ro the **r**erry-o,
The **rabbit** is in the mitten.

Additional verses: Replace bolded words with other animals and replace the bolded sounds with the initial sound in the animal's name. For example, *Bi-bo the berry-o, the **bear** is in the mitten.*

Winter Phonemic Awareness Songs & Rhymes © 1998 Creative Teaching Press

Polar Bear, Polar Bear

(sing to the tune of "Twinkle, Twinkle Little Star")

Polar Bear,

What do you hear?

I hear a **/p/** sound in my ear.

Do you hear a **/p/** in **fish?**

No, there's not a **/p/** in **fish.**

Do you hear a **/p/** in **penguin?**

Yes, I hear a **/p/** in **penguin.**

Additional verses: Replace bolded animals with different animals and the bolded sound with the initial sound in the animal's name. For example, *Seal, Seal, what do you hear? I hear a /s/ sound in my ear.*

Winter Phonemic Awareness Songs & Rhymes © 1998 Creative Teaching Press

♫♪ Peter the Penguin ♪♫

(sing to the tune of "On Top of Old Smokey")

Meet **Peter** the **Penguin.**

He munches on **Ps.**

If he eats the wrong food,

It might make him sneeze.

He likes **popcorn** and **pizza**

And **pineapple,** too.

What will you serve him

If he eats with you?

Note: Have students respond with other foods starting with the bolded letter.
Additional verses: Replace the bolded words to continue the song. For example, *Meet **Taylor** the **Tiger.** He munches on* **Ts.** *If he eats the wrong food, it might make him sneeze. He likes **tacos** and **tuna** and **tangerines,** too.*

Polar Play
Phoneme Substitution

Materials

- "Who Can Find the Polar Bear?" song (page 32)
- construction paper
- crayons or markers
- scissors
- glue
- tongue depressors

Have students draw on construction paper the face of a polar bear, whale, penguin, or seal and cut it out to make a mask. Invite students to cut out the eyes and glue a tongue depressor to the bottom of their mask. Ask four students, each with a different mask, to come to the front of the class to sing the appropriate part in "Who Can Find the Polar Bear?"

(Use with "Who Can Find the Polar Bear?" page 32)

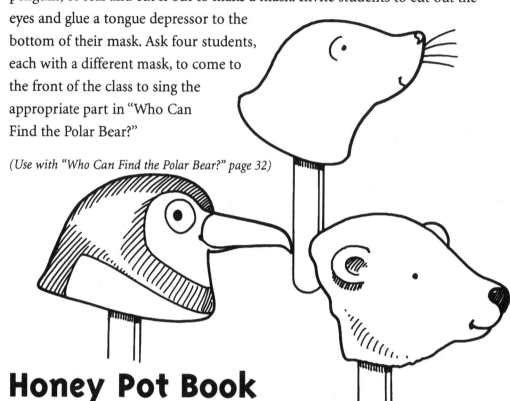

Honey Pot Book
Rhyming

Materials

- "Little Brown Bear" song (page 33)
- construction paper
- crayons or markers
- stapler

Have each student draw on construction paper a picture of where they would look for honey. Write the sentence frame *I left my cave looking for _____, but all I found _____!* Have students fill in the first blank with the name of where they would look and fill in the second blank with a rhyming word or phrase. For example, *I left my cave looking for <u>a hole</u>, but all I found <u>was a little gray mole!</u>* Staple the pages at the top to make a class flip-up book. Include for the last page a picture of a honey pot. Sing "Little Brown Bear" with your class and then ask students where the honey could be.

(Use with "Little Brown Bear," page 33)

Arctic Animal Match
Sound Matching

Enlarge the Arctic Animals reproducible, decorate each animal, cut it out, and glue it to a paper grocery sack. Have students cut out from magazines pictures of items that begin with /p/, /s/, and /b/. Have students place in each sack pictures that match the same initial sound. Ask students if they can think of more items that have the same initial sound as the animal on the sack.

(Use with "Arctic Pals," page 34)

Materials

● Arctic Animals reproducible (page 86)

● crayons or markers

● glue

● paper grocery sacks

● scissors

● magazines

Rhyme a Riddle
Rhyming

Mount copies of the Polar Animal Picture Cards on colored construction paper, laminate them, and give one card to each student. Write the words to "Antarctica Riddles" on sentence strips and place them in a pocket chart.

Invite student volunteers to place the correct picture cards in the pocket chart as the class sings "Antarctica Riddles." Vary this activity by having students hold up the picture card that answers the riddle. For an added challenge, invite students to write riddles about additional animals to continue the song.

(Use with "Antarctica Riddles," page 35)

Materials

● "Antarctica Riddles" song (page 35)

● Polar Animal Picture Cards (page 87)

● construction paper

● sentence strips

● pocket chart

Talk Like an Animal
Phoneme Substitution

Materials

● "Talking Animals"
  song (page 36)

● paper plates

● art supplies

Invite students to create paper-plate masks of either a reindeer, moose, or deer. While singing "Talking Animals," have students stand during their animal's part of the song and sing in their own "special" way.

(Use with "Talking Animals," page 36)

Move inside the Mitten
Phoneme Substitution

Materials

● "The Mitten" song
  (page 37)

● *The Mitten* by Jan Brett
  (Putnam)

● old sheet or blanket

Read aloud *The Mitten*. Create a large "mitten" from an old sheet or blanket. Choose different students to pretend to be each of the animals from the story— mole, rabbit, hedgehog, owl, badger, fox, bear, and mouse. As the class sings "The Mitten," the appropriate "animal" goes in the mitten (under the sheet or blanket). Continue until all the animals are in the mitten.

(Use with "The Mitten," page 37)

What Do You Hear?
Sound Matching

Have students draw different animals and use them to make paper-sack puppets. Invite student volunteers to help their puppet "sing" its part in "Polar Bear, Polar Bear." Replace the bolded animal name in the first line with the name of an animal puppet. Invite the class to ask the questions and have the volunteer respond. For example,

Class: **Walrus, Walrus,**
What do you hear?

Student: I hear a **/w/** sound in my ear.

Class: Do you hear a **/w/** in **dog?**

Student: No, there's not a **/w/** in **dog.**

(Use with "Polar Bear, Polar Bear," page 38)

I hear a /w/ sound in my ear.

Materials

● "Polar Bear, Polar Bear" song (page 38)

● paper sacks

● art supplies

Penguin Puppets
Sound Matching

Have students decorate and cut out the Peter Penguin reproducible. Have each student glue the penguin to a paper lunch sack. Have students color and cut out only the foods on the Fish Food Picture Cards that start with the **/p/** sound. Invite students to "feed" the fish food to the penguin while singing "Peter the Penguin."

(Use with "Peter the Penguin," page 39)

Materials

● "Peter the Penguin" song (page 39)

● Peter Penguin reproducible (page 88)

● Fish Food Picture Cards (page 89)

● art supplies

● scissors

● glue

● paper lunch sacks

Eating through the Week

(sing to the tune of "The Bear Went Over the Mountain")

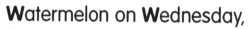

We can name the days.

We can name the days.

We can name the days

In the week ahead.

We eat **m**uffins on **M**onday,

Tacos on **T**uesday,

Watermelon on **W**ednesday,

As we eat through the days of the week.

We'll be **th**irsty on **Th**ursday,

Eat **f**rench **f**ries on **F**riday,

Soup on **S**aturday,

And **s**paghetti on **S**unday.

When It's Cold Outside

(sing to the tune of "Down by the Bay")

When it's cold outside,
And you want to play,
What can you do
For fun that day?
"Let's make a rhyme,"
My teacher would say.

Did you ever see a **snowflake** pushing a **rake**
On a cold winter's day?

When it's cold outside,
And you want to play,
What can you do
For fun that day?
"Let's make a rhyme,"
My teacher would say.

Did you ever see a polar **bear** combing his **hair**
On a cold winter's day?

Additional verses: Create additional rhymes to continue the song. For example, *Did you ever see a **bunny** eating jam and **honey?** Did you ever see a **bee** trying to **ski?** Did you ever see a **bed** turn into a **sled?** Did you ever see a **snowplow** taking a **bow?***

♫ Tell Me the Sound ♫

(sing to the tune of "Do Your Ears Hang Low?")

Tell me the first sound

That you can clearly hear.

Can you say it really loud?

Can you say it really clear?

When I say my special word,

Say the first sound that you hear.

What's the first sound you hear in **winter?**

Tell me the last sound

That you can clearly hear.

Can you say it really loud?

Can you say it really clear?

When I say my special word,

Say the last sound that you hear.

What's the last sound you hear in **winter?**

Note: Have students respond after each stanza.
Additional verses: Replace bolded words to continue the song.
For example, *What's the first sound you hear in **snow?***

♫ Winter First Sounds ♫

(sing to the tune of "Someone's in the Kitchen with Dinah")

What's the first sound you hear in **snowman?**

What's the first sound you hear in **snow?**

What's the first sound you hear in **sleet?**

The first sound we hear is **/s/.**

So we sing

Se, **s**i, **s**iddley-i-o,

Se, **s**i, **s**iddley-i-o-o-o-o.

Se, **s**i, siddley-i-o,

The first sound was **/s/.**

What's the last sound you hear in **cold?**

What's the last sound you hear in **sled?**

What's the last sound you hear in **snowed?**

The last sound we hear is **/d/.**

So we sing

De, **d**i, **d**iddley-i-o,

De, **d**i, **d**iddley-i-o-o-o-o.

De, **d**i, **d**iddley-i-o.

The last sound was **/d/.**

Additional verses: Replace bolded words with other winter words to continue the song. For example, *What's the first sound you hear in* **frost?** *What's the first sound you hear in* **freeze?** *What's the first sound you hear in* **fog?** Wait for the class to identify the beginning sound, then sing the chorus, substituting that initial sound.

♪ Mr. Snowman ♪

(sing to the tune of "This Old Man")

Mr. Snowman

Sings **/p/** songs.

He sings **/p/** songs all day long.

With a **p**ick-**p**ack-**p**addy-**p**ack

Sing his silly song.

He wants you to sing along.

Mr. Snowman

Sings **/ch/** songs.

He sings **/ch/** songs all day long.

With a **ch**ick-**ch**ack-**ch**addy-**ch**ack

Sing his silly song.

He wants you to sing along.

Mr. Snowman

Sings **/t/** songs.

He sings **/t/** songs all day long.

With a **t**ick-**t**ack-**t**addy-**t**ack

Sing his silly song.

He wants you to sing along.

Additional verses: Replace bolded phonemes to continue the song. For example, *Mr. Snowman sings /s/ songs. He sings /s/ songs all day long. With a sick-sack-saddy-sack sing his silly song.*

Winter Phonemic Awareness Songs & Rhymes © 1998 Creative Teaching Press

♫ Sound Soup ♫

(sing to the tune of "When the Saints Go Marching In")

What can you add

To our sound soup?

What can you add to our sound soup?

It must begin with the sound **/b/**

To belong in our sound soup.

We can add **beets.**

We can add **broccoli.**

We can even add some **basil.**

They all begin with the sound **/b/**

And make a very tasty soup.

Additional verses: Replace the bolded sounds and foods to continue the song. For example,
*We can add turnips. We can add **tomatoes.** We can even add some **tangerines.***

Eating Every Day
Sound Matching

Write the days of the week on sentence strips, hole-punch the top of each strip, and use straight pins to place them near your calendar. Have students brainstorm food items that begin with the same sound as each day of the week and draw them on sentence strips. Each day, sing "Eating through the Week," and invite a student to uncover the new day and the food items that begin with the same sound.

(Use with "Eating through the Week," page 44)

Let's Make a Rhyme Book
Rhyming

Ask students to illustrate different rhymes from "When It's Cold Outside," such as a snowflake pushing a rake. Invite each student to create a silly rhyme drawing. As students sing their rhyme, have them hold up their drawing. Then combine the drawings into a class big book.

(Use with "When It's Cold Outside," page 45)

Name Game
Sound Matching, Phoneme Isolation

After the class sings "Tell Me the Sound" using different winter-related words, try replacing the winter words with students' names. Hold up student photos as visuals or just call students by name. Challenge the children to name all the students whose names begin with the same sound. Ask students if they can think of other words that begin with the same first sound as the name.

(Use with "Tell Me the Sound," page 46)

Materials

- "Tell Me the Sound" song (page 46)
- student photos (optional)

How Many Sounds?
Syllable Counting, Phoneme Counting

Divide the class into four groups. Give each group ace through ten playing cards of one suit. Tell students that the ace stands for the number one. Sing "Tell Me the Sound" with your class. Ask each group to hold up a playing card to show how many syllables or how many sounds are in the final word of the song. For example, if you ask students how many syllables are in *winter,* students would hold up the two of their suit (win-ter). If you ask how many sounds are in *snow,* students would hold up the three of their suit (/s/ /n/ /o/).

(Use with "Tell Me the Sound," page 46)

Materials

- "Tell Me the Sound" song (page 46)
- playing cards

Snowball Toss
Sound Matching

Materials

● white paper

Have each student write one letter in the center of a white sheet of paper. Invite students to crumble their paper to create a "snowball." Have students stand in a circle. Say *Snowball, snowball, in the snow. Let's make them fall when I say "go."* Students toss their snowball into the air after you say *go.* Each student collects one snowball and sits in the circle. Each student then names the letter on the paper, makes the sound, and names an object that begins with that sound.

(Use with "Winter First Sounds," page 47)

Singing Snow Kids
Phoneme Substitution

Materials

● "Mr. Snowman" song (page 48)

● paper plates

● scissors

● black construction paper

● stapler

● hole punch

● black yarn

● white crayons

Give each student a paper plate. Help students cut a 6" (15 cm) hole in the center of their plate. Show students how to roll large black construction paper into a cylinder and fit it into the paper-plate opening to make a top hat. Have students staple the cylinder so it stays closed. Then have students punch a hole on each side of their plate and tie black yarn to each side. Ask students to write a letter with white crayon on their hat. Invite students to wear their top hat. Choose a few students to stand in front of the class and be "snow kids." Have the class sing "Mr. Snowman," substituting the letter on each snow kid's hat. As students finish singing each student's sound, the student "melts" to the ground.

(Use with "Mr. Snowman," page 48)

Pass the Pot

Sound Matching

Have each student draw on a blank index card a picture of a food item that can go in soup. Discuss the drawings and invite students to place their drawing into a large soup pot or kettle. Ask students to sit in a circle. Pass the pot around and have each student choose one "food" item from the pot. Place the pot in the center of the circle. As you sing "Sound Soup," the students with foods that start with the designated sound return their item to the pot.

(Use with "Sound Soup," page 49)

Materials

- "Sound Soup" song (page 49)
- blank index cards
- art supplies
- large soup pot or kettle

Making Sound Soup

Sound Matching

Send home a photocopy of the family letter with each student. On the day the students bring the food, have them sort the food by initial sound. Then invite each student to add his or her food to a slow cooker while saying the first sound it makes and the corresponding letter. When all foods are in the pot, stir them up, cook, and enjoy.

(Use with "Sound Soup," page 49)

Materials

- family letter (page 90)
- slow cooker
- bowls and spoons

What Will I Wear in Winter?

(sing to the tune of "Down by the Bay")

It's snowing outside,

And I need to get dressed.

I need my /c/ /a/ /p/

And my /sc/ /ar/ /f/.

I need my /c/ /oa/ /t/

And my mit-tens, too.

Next, I need my /b/ /oo/ /t/ /s/

To play with you!

Note: Have students pretend to put on each clothing item as each word is segmented.

Mom's Mixed Up

(sing to the tune of "The Farmer in the Dell")

It's raining outside, it's raining outside.

My mom said, "Put on your oots."

So I put on my **boots.**

It's snowing outside, it's snowing outside.

My mom said, "Put on your **ittens.**"

So I put on my **mittens.**

It's windy outside, it's windy outside.

My mom said, "Put on your **acket.**"

So I put on my **jacket.**

It's sunny outside, it's sunny outside.

My mom said, "Take off your **arf.**"

So I took off my **scarf.**

Note: Have students put on (or pretend to put on) each clothing item after each stanza, and have students remove the items after the last stanza.

Additional verses: Replace the bolded rime (word ending) to continue the song. For example, *My mom said, "Put on your **icker.**" So I put on my **slicker.*** Pause for students to add the missing onset and say the word.

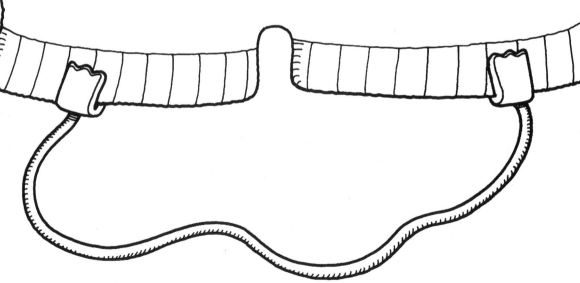

Colorful Mittens

(sing to the tune of "Six Little Ducks")

Colorful mittens for me and you.

Red ones, yellow ones, blue ones, too.

But the one pair of mittens that rhymes with **fellow,**

They're my favorite mittens.

They're the color **yellow.**

Additional verses: Have students replace bolded words to continue the song.
For example, *But the one pair of mittens that rhymes with* **bed,** *they're my*
favorite mittens. They're the color **red.**

Winter Phonemic Awareness Songs & Rhymes © 1998 Creative Teaching Press

Can You Find My Mitten?

(sing to the tune of "The Muffin Man")

Oh, can you find my **mitten**,

My **mitten**, my **mitten**?

Oh, can you find my **mitten**?

It's **/r/ /e/ /d/**.

Additional verses: Have students replace bolded words and phonemes to continue the song. For example, *Oh, can you find my **jacket**? It's **str—iped**.*

What Will We Wear?   **57**

Rainy Weather

(sing to the tune of "The Muffin Man")

What do you wear in **rainy** weather,

Rainy weather, **rainy** weather?

What do you wear in **rainy** weather?

Do you wear a **h—at?**

Note: Have students answer the question at the end of the song and pretend to put on the item.

Additional verses: Have students replace bolded words and phonemes to continue the song. For example, *What do you wear in **snowy** weather? Do you wear **sh—orts?***

♫ Little Snowman ♫

(sing to the tune of "One Little Elephant")

One little snowman went out to play on a snowy winter's day.

He went out looking for his **at**.

Some friends came by and brought his **hat**.

Two little snowmen went out to play on a snowy winter's day.

They went out looking for their **arves**.

Some friends came by and brought their **scarves**.

Three little snowmen went out to play on a snowy winter's day.

They went out looking for their **ittens**.

Some friends came by and brought their **mittens**.

Four little snowmen went out to play on a snowy winter's day.

They went out looking for their **oots**.

Some friends came by and brought their **boots**.

Five little snowmen went out to play on a snowy winter's day.

They went out looking for their **ooms**.

Some friends came by and brought their **brooms**.

Note: Pause for students to add the beginning sound(s) to the bolded word at the end of each stanza.

Dress Up
Phoneme Counting, Phoneme Segmentation

Materials

● "What Will I Wear in Winter?" song (page 54)

● scissors

● felt

● sentence strips

● flannel board

Cut the following winter clothing items from felt: a cap, a scarf, a coat, mittens, and boots. Write the clothing words on sentence strips and cut apart the letters. Make a felt person to be used on a flannel board. After the class sings "What Will I Wear in Winter?" have students put the clothing items on the felt person as they segment and count the sounds. For example, coat has three phonemes: /c/ /oa/ /t/.

(Use with "What Will I Wear in Winter?" page 54)

What Should I Wear?
Syllable Counting, Phoneme Counting, Phoneme Segmentation, Phoneme Addition

Materials

● "Mom's Mixed Up" song (page 55)

● winter clothing (boots, mittens, a jacket, and a sweater)

Bring winter clothing to school. Invite a student volunteer to stand in front of the class to "dress for the weather." As the class sings "Mom's Mixed Up," invite the class to identify the correct clothing item for the student to put on. Have the volunteer count the number of phonemes or syllables in the word as he or she puts on the item. Sing the song again while the student takes off each item. For a greater challenge, invite students to segment the words. For example, *My mom said, "Put on your /b/ /oo/ /t/ /s/."*

(Use with "Mom's Mixed Up," page 55)

Rhyming Mittens

Rhyming

In advance, cut out assorted colors of construction-paper mittens using the Mittens reproducible as a pattern. Write a color word on each one. Give each student a mitten, sing "Colorful Mittens," and have students hold up their mitten when their rhyme is sung. For additional practice, invite students to draw a picture of an item that rhymes with their color word on the back side of the mitten.

(Use with "Colorful Mittens," page 56)

Materials

- "Colorful Mittens" song (page 56)
- Mittens reproducible (page 91)
- scissors
- construction paper (assorted colors)

Find the Mitten, Pick It Up

Phoneme Blending

In advance, cut out assorted colors of construction-paper mittens using the Mittens reproducible as a pattern. Have students hold hands and make a circle. Place the mittens at the students' feet and as the class sings "Can You Find My Mitten?" have students walk around the circle. At the end of the song, the child who is standing in front of the chosen color picks it up and shows the class.

(Use with "Can You Find My Mitten?" page 57)

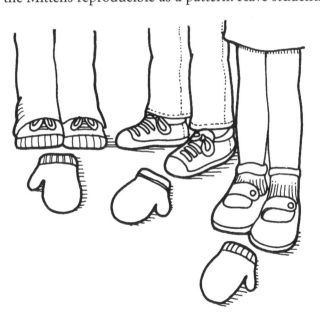

Materials

- "Can You Find My Mitten?" song (page 57)
- Mittens reproducible (page 91)
- scissors
- construction paper (assorted colors)

Dressing Room
Syllable Counting, Phoneme Blending, Phoneme Counting

In advance, write numbers on separate index cards, hole-punch the top of each card, and string yarn through the hole to make necklaces. Place clothing items worn during various types of weather in a basket. Sing "Rainy Weather" with the class, and invite a volunteer to blend the word and choose that item from the basket. Ask another volunteer to say the word and count the syllables or (for a greater challenge) count the phonemes. Then have the volunteer choose a necklace with the correct number of syllables or phonemes and place it on the child wearing the clothing item.

(Use with "Rainy Weather," page 58)

Dress the Snowman
Phoneme Addition

Trace on construction paper all the patterns from the Snowman reproducible. Cut out the patterns, including five copies of the snowman pattern. Attach magnetic tape to the back of each shape. Let the students place the items on the magnetic board as the class sings "Little Snowman."

(Use with "Little Snowman," page 59)

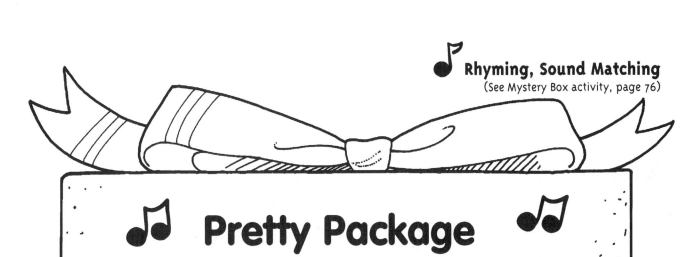

Pretty Package

(sing to the tune of "Where, Oh, Where Has My Little Dog Gone?")

I wonder what's in the pretty package.

I wonder what's in it for me.

It starts with /**b**/

And it rhymes with **hair.**

What do you think it could be?

I wonder what's in the pretty package.

I wonder what's in it for me.

It starts with /**t**/

And it rhymes with **boy.**

What do you think it could be?

I wonder what's in the pretty package.

I wonder what's in it for me.

It starts with /**w**/

And it rhymes with **dragon.**

What do you think it could be?

Additional verses: Replace the bolded sounds and words to continue the song. For example, *It starts with /**b**/ and it rhymes with **tall.** What do you think it could be?*

Jolly Old Santa

(sing to the tune of "I'm a Little Teapot")

I'm a little Santa, jolly and fat.

Here is my beard, and here is my hat.

Early Christmas evening, I will pack

Lots of goodies in my sack.

Put the **/s/** toys in the back.

What are some that I might lack?

Note: Have students respond with toys that begin with the bolded sound.

Additional verses: Replace the bolded sound to continue the song. For example, *Put the **/b/** toys in the back.*

Winter Phonemic Awareness Songs & Rhymes © 1998 Creative Teaching Press

♪ Santa's Helpers ♪

(sing to the tune of "Down by the Station")

In Santa's workshop,

Late in the evening

Listen to his funny elves

Playing with their sounds.

Change a name to start with **/sh/.**

Change **Kelsey** to start with **/sh/.**

Shelsey   **/sh/.**

Shelsey   **/sh/.**

What's the name?

Shout it now. . . .

Additional verses: Replace the bolded name and sounds to continue the song.
For example, *Change a name to start with* **/t/.**

♫ # Holiday Packages ♫

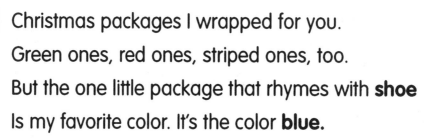

(sing to the tune of "Six Little Ducks")

Christmas packages I wrapped for you.

Green ones, red ones, striped ones, too.

But the one little package that rhymes with **shoe**

Is my favorite color. It's the color **blue.**

Christmas packages I wrapped for you.

Green ones, red ones, striped ones, too.

But the one little package that rhymes with **bed**

Is my favorite color. It's the color **red.**

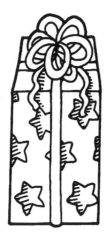

Additional verses: Replace the bolded words to continue the song. For example, *But the one little package that rhymes with* **ink** *is my favorite color. It's the color* **pink.**

(See Piñata Prizes activity, page 78)

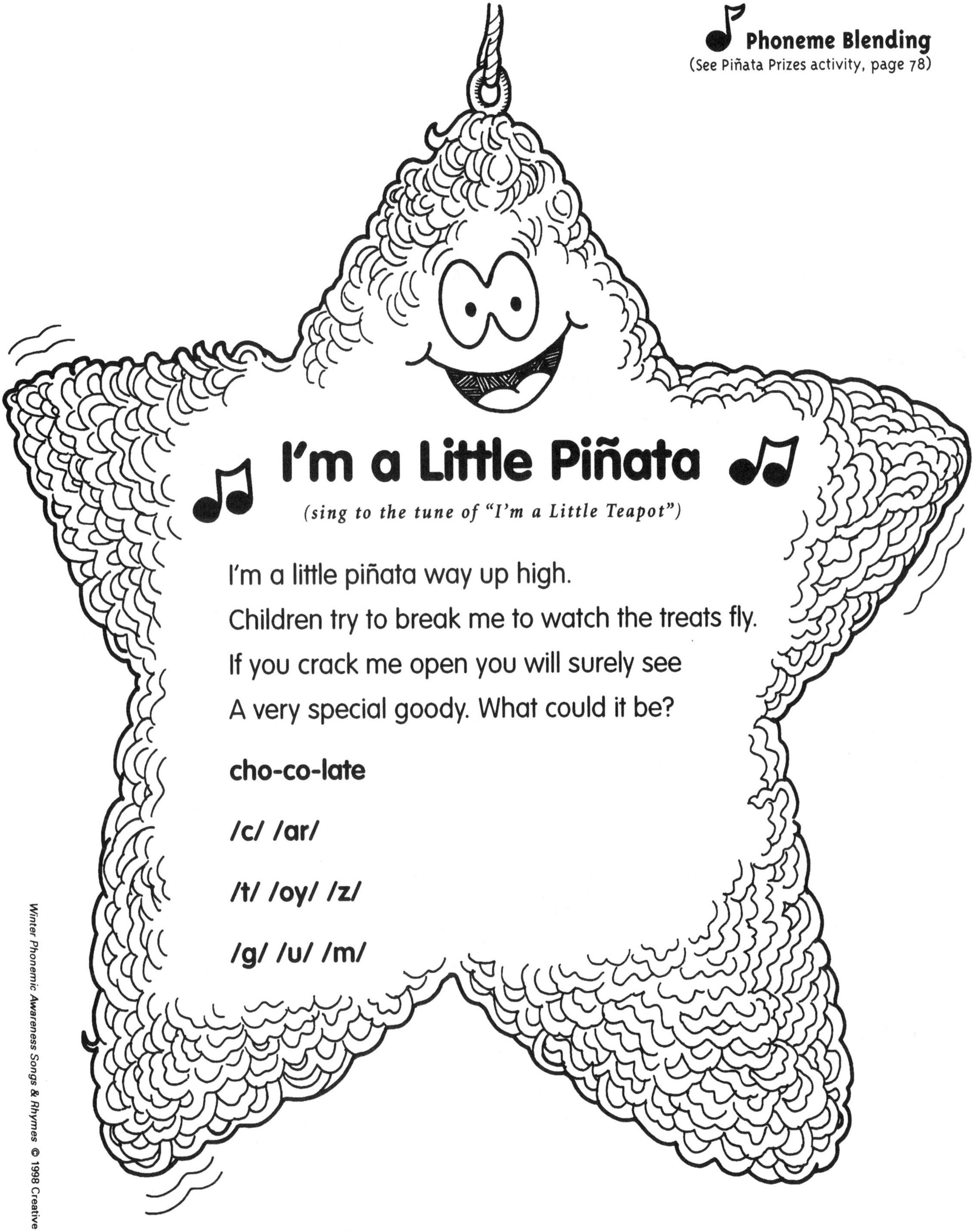

I'm a Little Piñata

(sing to the tune of "I'm a Little Teapot")

I'm a little piñata way up high.
Children try to break me to watch the treats fly.
If you crack me open you will surely see
A very special goody. What could it be?

cho-co-late

/c/ /ar/

/t/ /oy/ /z/

/g/ /u/ /m/

Note: Pause for students to blend each set of phonemes.
Additional verses: Replace bolded phonemes to continue the song.

The Gingerbread Man

(sing to the tune of "The Wheels on the Bus")

The gingerbread man ran through the town,
Through the town, through the town.
The gingerbread man ran through the town,
Singing, "You will never catch me."

He ran away from a **/c/ /ow/,**
/c/ /ow/   /c/ /ow/.
He ran away from a **cow,**
Singing, "You will never catch me."

He ran away from a **/sh/ /ee/ /p/,**
/sh/ /ee/ /p/   /sh/ /ee/ /p/.
He ran from a **sheep** without a peep,
Singing, "You will never catch me."

He ran away from a **/d/ /o/ /g/,**
/d/ /o/ /g/   /d/ /o/ /g/.
He ran away from a **dog,**
Singing, "You will never catch me."

Then he came to a **/f/ /o/ /x/,**
/f/ /o/ /x/   /f/ /o/ /x/.
The **fox** sat on a box and said,
"You can trust me."
Then he ate him, yes sir-ee.

Note: Pause for students to blend each set of phonemes.

You can trust me.

♫ I'm a Little Groundhog

(sing to the tune of "I'm a Little Teapot")

I'm a little groundhog, furry and round.

You may see me pop out of the ground.

If I see my shadow, down I'll stay.

Six more weeks of winter's on its way.

I know a little game, won't you play with me?

Look around the room. What do you see?

When I see something that starts with **/p/,**

I pop up on the count of three.

Note: After students see and say an item that begins with the bolded sound, have them pop up on the count of three.

Additional verses: Replace bolded sound to continue the song. For example, *When I see something that starts with **/g/,** I pop up on the count of three.*

♫ **Valentines** ♫

(sing to the tune of "Six Little Ducks")

Five little valentines that I once knew
Red ones, blue ones, yellow ones, too.
But the valentine that rhymes with **ink**
Is my favorite color. It's the color **pink!**

Additional verses: Replace bolded words to continue the song. For example, *But the valentine that rhymes with* **queen** *is my favorite color. It's the color* **green!**

Winter Phonemic Awareness Songs & Rhymes © 1998 Creative Teaching Press

Can You Find My Valentine?

(sing to the tune of "The Muffin Man")

Can you find my valentine,

Valentine, valentine?

Can you find my valentine?

It looks **/l/ /a/ /c/ /y/**.

Additional verses: Replace bolded phonemes to continue the song. For example,
It looks /f/ /u/ /n/ /ee/. Have students blend the sounds to describe the valentine.

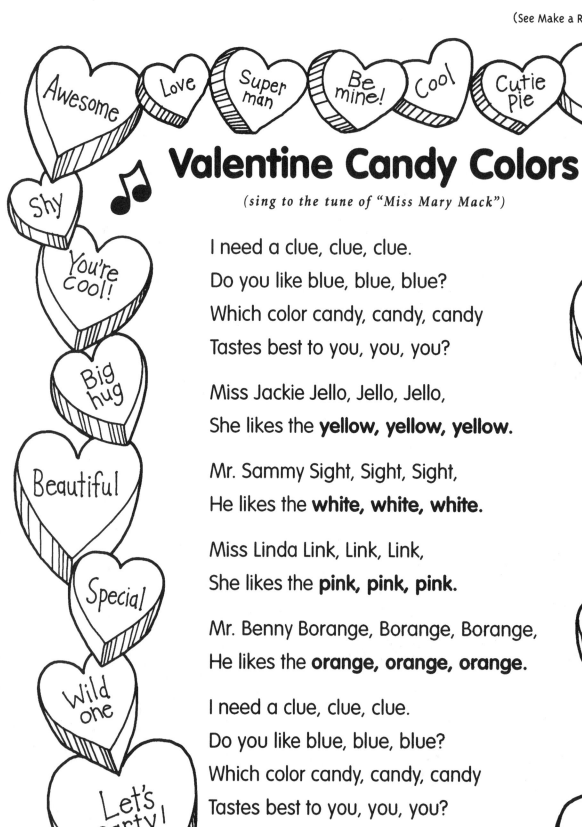

Valentine Candy Colors

(sing to the tune of "Miss Mary Mack")

I need a clue, clue, clue.

Do you like blue, blue, blue?

Which color candy, candy, candy

Tastes best to you, you, you?

Miss Jackie Jello, Jello, Jello,

She likes the **yellow, yellow, yellow.**

Mr. Sammy Sight, Sight, Sight,

He likes the **white, white, white.**

Miss Linda Link, Link, Link,

She likes the **pink, pink, pink.**

Mr. Benny Borange, Borange, Borange,

He likes the **orange, orange, orange.**

I need a clue, clue, clue.

Do you like blue, blue, blue?

Which color candy, candy, candy

Tastes best to you, you, you?

Note: Pause for students to say the bolded rhyming color word.

Winter Phonemic Awareness Songs & Rhymes © 1998 Creative Teaching Press

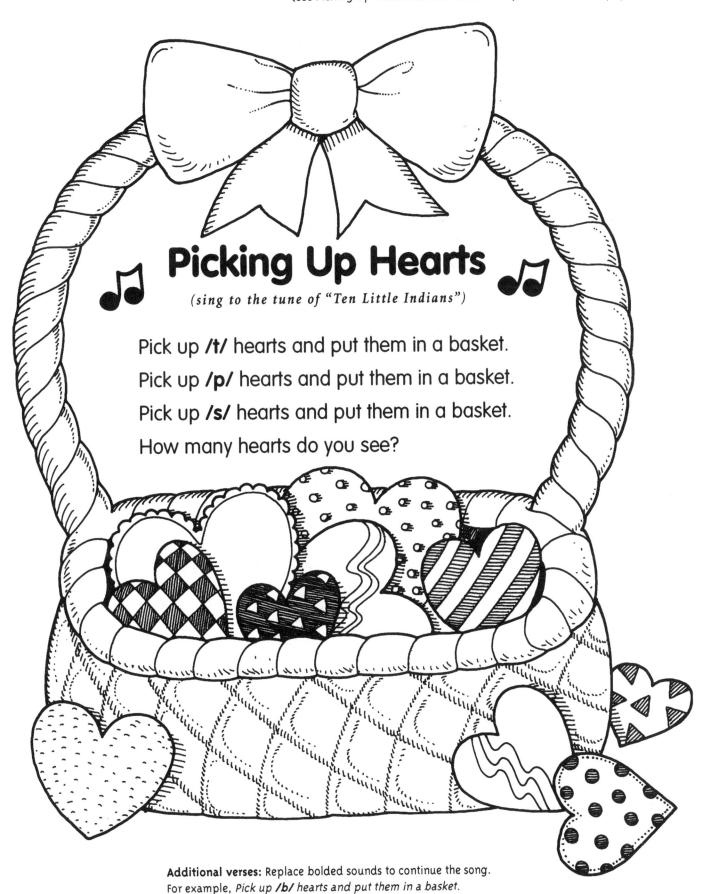

Picking Up Hearts
(sing to the tune of "Ten Little Indians")

Pick up **/t/** hearts and put them in a basket.

Pick up **/p/** hearts and put them in a basket.

Pick up **/s/** hearts and put them in a basket.

How many hearts do you see?

Additional verses: Replace bolded sounds to continue the song.
For example, *Pick up /b/ hearts and put them in a basket.*

I Love Somebody

(sing to the tune of "Skip to My Lou")

I love somebody. Yes, I do.

I love somebody. Yes, I do.

I love somebody. Yes, I do.

Let me say it slow for you.

/E/ /m/ /i/ /l/ /ee/

Additional verses: Replace bolded set of phonemes to continue the song. Have students blend the name.

Pushing Pennies

(sing to the tune of "The Muffin Man")

Abraham Lincoln is on the penny.
He's on the front of every penny.
And he loved to play a penny game
Called Pushing Pennies.

I'll say a word, then I'll say it slowly.
You say the word very slowly.
Then you move a penny in the box
When you hear the sound.

Winter Phonemic Awareness Songs & Rhymes © 1998 Creative Teaching Press

Note: Say a word aloud, segmenting the sounds, and have students push a penny into small boxes drawn on paper for each phoneme they hear.

Mystery Box
Rhyming, Sound Matching

Materials

- "Pretty Package" song (page 63)
- plastic animals or toys
- fancy box with removable top

Hide plastic animals or toys in a fancy box with a removable top. Sing "Pretty Package," providing a rhyming word clue to one of the objects. When students tell you the name of the rhyming object, pull it out of the box for all to see. Continue until all objects have been taken out of the box.

(Use with "Pretty Package," page 63)

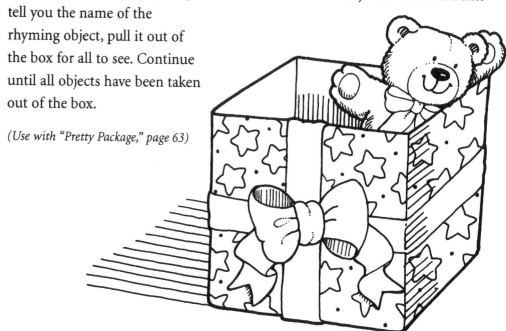

Santa Syllables
Sound Matching, Syllable Counting, Phoneme Counting

Materials

- "Jolly Old Santa" song (page 64)
- scrap paper
- beans or poker chips (optional)

Have students sing "Jolly Old Santa." List on the board the toys students contribute at the end of the song. Ask students to draw on scrap paper a line for each syllable they hear in a toy name. Then have students make a dot (or place a bean or poker chip) under each line for each sound they hear in each syllable. Walk around the room to monitor students' work. Tell students to "stretch" out the sounds in the word to hear each sound. Have students do the activity again with another word from the song.

(Use with "Jolly Old Santa," page 64)

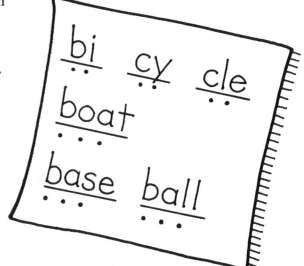

Elf Name Change
Phoneme Isolation, Phoneme Substitution

Write each student's name on an index card, cut apart the letters, and place them in a resealable plastic bag with a few extra letters. Have students place the letters on their desk and spell their name. Then ask students to replace the beginning sound of their name with a new sound. Observe students as they manipulate their name. For example, *Whitney* may change her name to *Bitney*. For a greater challenge, ask students to replace the ending sound of their name with a new sound. For example, *Taylor* could become *Taylee*.

(Use with "Santa's Helpers," page 65)

Materials

- index cards
- scissors
- resealable plastic bags

Pass the Package
Rhyming, Phoneme Segmentation

In advance, fill a small box with enough gummy bears for every child to get one. Wrap the box in several layers of different colored construction or tissue paper. Have students sit in a circle. Sing "Holiday Packages" with your class and pass the gift-wrapped package around the circle. When it comes time to sing a rhyming word, ask the student holding the package to say a word that rhymes with the color of the wrapping paper and then unwrap the top layer of wrapping paper. Have the class continue passing the package and singing the song. When the last layer of wrapping paper is removed, treat all players to a gummy bear. Before they eat it, have students segment the sounds of their color.

(Use with "Holiday Packages," page 66)

Materials

- "Holiday Packages" song (page 66)
- gummy bears
- small box
- construction paper or tissue paper (assorted solid colors)

Piñata Prizes

Phoneme Blending, Phoneme Segmentation

Place in a basket a variety of small prizes that could be found in a piñata, such as small toys, treats, and candies. Blindfold a volunteer and have him or her choose an item from the basket and hold it up. Ask the rest of the class to separate the sounds of the object, and have the volunteer blend the sounds to

guess the object. For example, if the volunteer holds up a little flag, the class would say /f/ /l/ /a/ /g/. Then the blindfolded student would blend the phonemes and say *flag*. Blindfold a new volunteer to continue the game.

(Use with "I'm a Little Piñata," page 67)

You Can't Catch Me!

Phoneme Counting, Phoneme Segmentation

Hold up a farm animal picture or object and ask the class to segment the sounds of the animal's name by tapping progressively at up to five points up their arms to their head (fingers, wrist, elbow, shoulder, and head). For example, if you held up a small plastic pig, students would tap their fingers, wrist, then elbow while saying /p/ /i/ /g/. Then ask students how many phonemes they heard in the word. By tapping their body parts, they can visually see how many phonemes are in the word.

(Use with "The Gingerbread Man," page 68)

Goofy Groundhog
Sound Matching, Phoneme Counting

Have students color and cut out the Groundhog reproducible. Invite students to glue the groundhog on a drinking straw. Then have students poke a hole in the bottom of a Styrofoam cup. Have students glue raffia or Spanish moss to the rim of the cup. Read a word from "I'm a Little Groundhog" slowly so students can hear each sound, and invite students to poke their straw through the cup hole to pop their groundhog up for every sound they hear. Ask students to count the number of times Mr. Groundhog pops up for various words. For sound matching practice, invite a volunteer to pop up his or her groundhog and say a sound such as /b/. Then invite the rest of the class to pop up their groundhog so he is looking at an object in the room that begins with that sound.

(Use with "I'm a Little Groundhog," page 69)

Materials

- "I'm a Little Groundhog" song (page 69)
- Groundhog reproducible (page 93)
- crayons or markers
- scissors
- glue
- drinking straws
- Styrofoam cups
- raffia or Spanish moss

Valentine Hearts
Rhyming

In advance, write color words and words that rhyme with color words on separate construction-paper hearts. Distribute a heart to each student. Sing "Valentines" with the class and have the student whose word is sung stand and then the student with the rhyming color word stands. Continue singing until all students participate.

(Use with "Valentines," page 70)

Materials

- "Valentines" song (page 70)
- construction-paper hearts

Valentine Fun

Phoneme Blending, Phoneme Segmentation

In advance, display valentines around the room. Sing "Can You Find My Valentine?" with your class. At the end of the song, segment the sounds in a word that describes one of the valentines displayed. Ask students to blend the sounds and point to the valentine you described. For a greater challenge, invite a student to segment the sounds in a word describing one of the valentines, and have the rest of the class blend the sounds and point to the correct valentine.

(Use with "Can You Find My Valentine?" page 71)

Make a Rhyme

Rhyming

Give each student a resealable plastic bag with candy conversation hearts. Have students sort conversation hearts by color. Then sing "Valentine Candy Colors" with the class and ask students what color each character likes best. After singing the song and making rhymes, have each student count the number of candies for each color. Ask students questions such as *Did you find more yellow or pink hearts?* Brainstorm other words that rhyme with color words and rewrite the song using the new rhyming words. Sing the last part of the song one more time and invite students to eat their favorite colored candies. Have students put the rest of the candies back in their bag. Staple a copy of the song to each bag and have students take it home to share with their family.

(Use with "Valentine Candy Colors," page 72)

Picking Up Valentines

Sound Matching

Collect valentines and place them in a basket. Have students sit in a circle. Place the basket in the middle of the circle and lay valentines (with the pictures facing up) around it. Sing "Picking Up Hearts" with the class and invite student volunteers to pick up valentines that have a picture with the same initial sound asked for in the song and place them in the basket. Each time the beginning sound changes, choose a new group of students to pick up valentines.

(Use with "Picking Up Hearts," page 73)

Materials

- "Picking Up Hearts" song (page 73)
- valentines
- basket

Basket Full of Hearts

Sound Matching

Have each student attach a pipe cleaner to a berry basket or paper sack to form a handle. Invite students to color and cut out the pictures on the Picking Up Hearts reproducible. Then have students sit in a circle with their pictures in front of them. As you sing "Picking Up Hearts" together, have students place the correct pictures in their basket. Attach a copy of the song to the basket and send it home for students to share with their family.

(Use with "Picking Up Hearts," page 73)

Materials

- "Picking Up Hearts" song (page 73)
- Picking Up Hearts reproducible (page 94)
- pipe cleaners
- plastic berry baskets or paper sacks
- crayons or markers
- scissors

I See Something
Phoneme Blending, Phoneme Segmentation

Materials

• "I Love Somebody" song (page 74)

Have all the children sit in a circle. Change the words from "I Love Somebody" to *I see something. Yes, I do.* Invite one child to think of something, segment the sounds of the word, and invite the rest of the class to blend the sounds and make a guess. Continue the game for all students to play.

(Use with "I Love Somebody," page 74)

Push a Penny
Phoneme Isolation, Phoneme Counting

Materials

• "Pushing Pennies" song (page 75)

• pennies

Give each student several pennies. Sing "Pushing Pennies" with your class and, at the end of the song, slowly call out a word, "stretching" out each sound. Have students push a penny forward on their desk for every sound they hear in the word. For example, the word *penny* has four sounds (/p/ /e/ /n/ /ee/), so each student would push four pennies forward to show the number of sounds.

(Use with "Pushing Pennies," page 75)

Rhyming Picture Cards

Winter Phonemic Awareness Songs & Rhymes © 1998 Creative Teaching Press

Rhyming Picture Cards

Polar Bear

Arctic Animals

Winter Phonemic Awareness Songs & Rhymes © 1998 Creative Teaching Press

Polar Animal Picture Cards

Peter Penguin

Winter Phonemic Awareness Songs & Rhymes © 1998 Creative Teaching Press

Fish Food Picture Cards

Dear Family,

We have been learning our letter sounds. To celebrate all the sounds we have learned, we will be making Sound Soup on _____. Please send one of the following items for our soup:

• chopped carrots, celery, onions, or tomatoes.

• canned or fresh peas, string beans, corn, potatoes, or pinto beans.

• a can of vegetable soup.

Thank you for helping us celebrate sounds!

Winter Phonemic Awareness Songs & Rhymes © 1998 Creative Teaching Press

Mittens

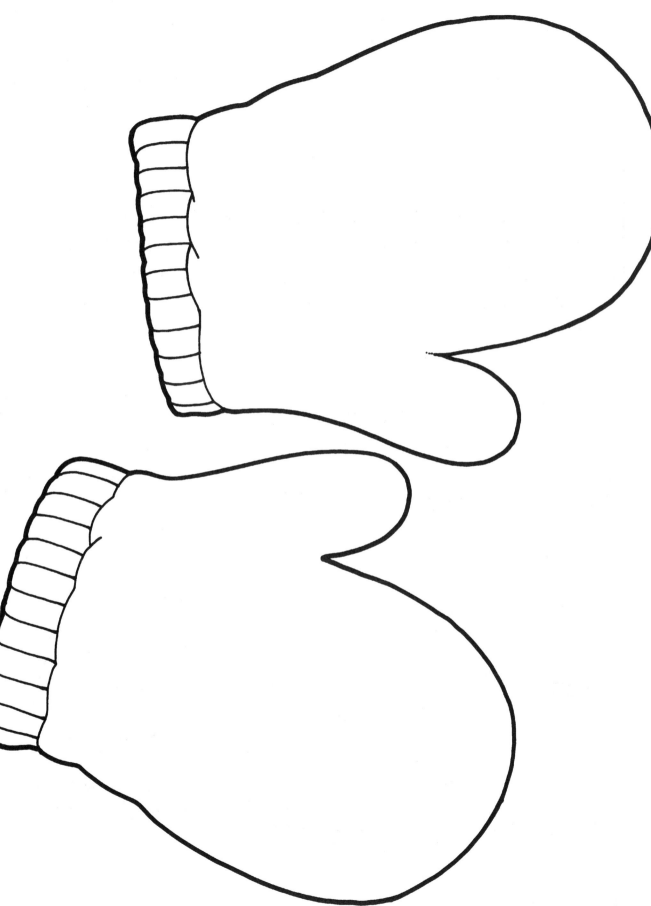

Snowman

Winter Phonemic Awareness Songs & Rhymes © 1998 Creative Teaching Press

Groundhog

Winter Phonemic Awareness Songs & Rhymes © 1998 Creative Teaching Press

Picking Up Hearts

Winter Phonemic Awareness Songs & Rhymes © 1998 Creative Teaching Press

Phonemic-Awareness Index

♫ *Song Title*

♪ *Song Title*